MARVELLOUS
MACHINES

SEE INSIDE MACHINES · WITH A MAGIC LENS

By **Jane Wilsher**

Illustrated by **Andrés Lozano**

Consultant: **Dr Joseph Corcoran,**
Imperial College London

What on Earth Books is an imprint of What on Earth Publishing
The Black Barn, Wickhurst Farm, Tonbridge, Kent TN11 8PS, United Kingdom
30 Ridge Road Unit B, Greenbelt, Maryland, 20770, United States

First published in the United Kingdom in 2021

Staff for this book: Editor, Patrick Skipworth; Art Director, Andy Forshaw;
Designer, Daisy Symes

Consultant: Dr Joseph Corcoran, Imperial College London, UK

A CIP catalogue record for this book is available from the British Library

ISBN: 978-1-9129201-9-8

Printed in China

10 9 8 7 6 5 4 3 2 1

whatonearthbooks.com

WHAT'S INSIDE

HOW TO USE THE MAGIC LENS

This book comes complete with an incredible invention – a magic lens that reveals the inner workings of the machines in the pictures.
In this book, whenever you see red speckled or criss-cross patterns, wave your lens over the pattern to reveal what's hidden. Why not try it on the box below?

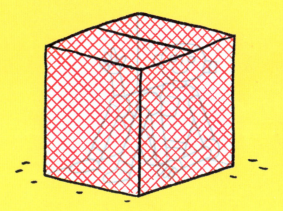

Can you see the robot inside the box? Try out the magic lens on all the pictures in this book. Look out for these picture clues.

When you see a picture of the magic lens, look at the picture through the lens to find out how things work.

When you see a picture of an eye, try to find all the machines, gizmos and gadgets on the numbered list. Some things you can see in the picture and some are hidden. You'll need your magic lens to spot the hidden things!

HOW THINGS WORK

What's a machine?

A machine can be as simple as a pencil sharpener or as complicated as a rocket that blasts into space. Machines make or do things quickly and easily.

Factories use combinations of machines to make lots of the things we use and rely on every day. Each machine has a task. The machines keep working until each piece is made and the job is done.

LOOK INSIDE
Find out how simple everyday machines work.

When you push a **lever** down, the force helps move something else up or down with a stronger force.

A **pulley** helps to move a heavy object upwards.

A **wheel** spins, or rotates, smoothly around a long bar called an **axle**.

Gears are sets of spinning wheels with teeth that fit together to move and turn each other.

A **screw** can lift up an object or hold things together. And it can wind and unwind.

What makes a machine go?

A force. Think of a force as a push or a pull that makes a machine start, move or go faster in one direction. Many forces are invisible. Here are some of the different types of forces you might come across:

Contact forces

These forces happen when two objects touch each other. When you pull or push a door, you provide a contact force to open the door.

Weight

Gravity pulls everything down to the ground. The pulling force is called weight and this is why objects feel heavy.

Friction

This force pulls everything back. When two surfaces rub together, friction makes it harder for them to move against each other.

Air resistance

This special type of friction pushes against things while they travel through the air. It's the force that slows a parachute down while it falls to the ground, or makes a windmill spin steadily in a breeze.

Magnetism

This force pulls and pushes certain objects together or apart, such as magnets or magnetic metals.

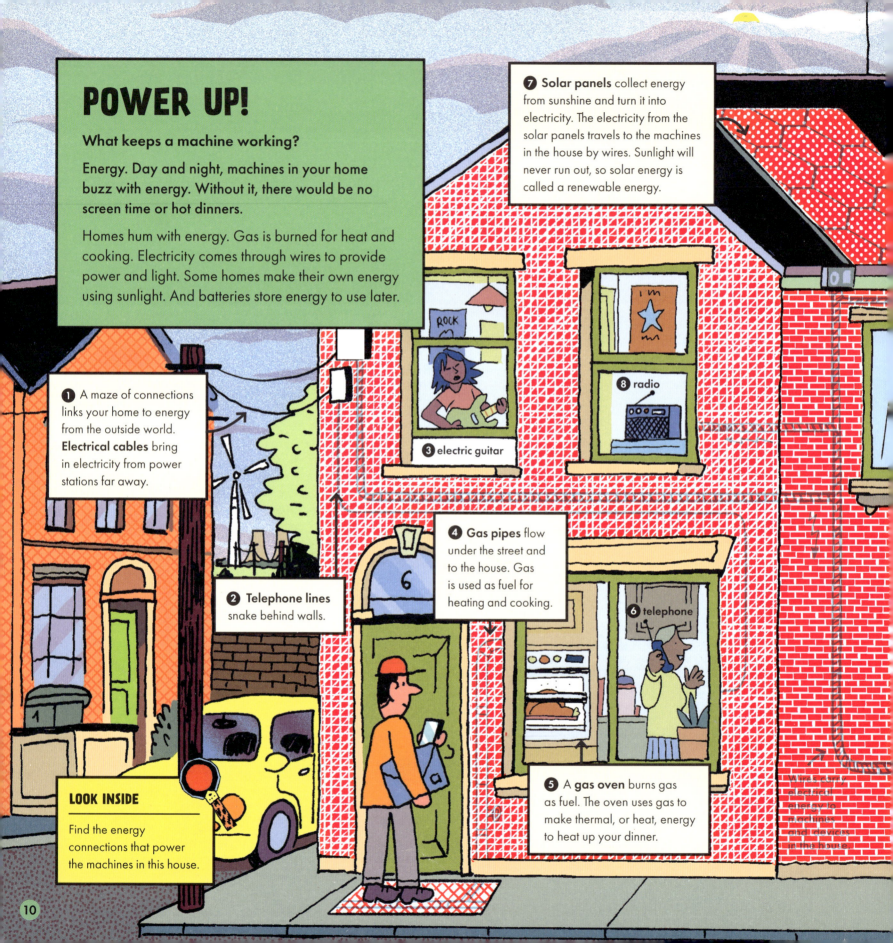

POWER UP!

What keeps a machine working?

Energy. Day and night, machines in your home buzz with energy. Without it, there would be no screen time or hot dinners.

Homes hum with energy. Gas is burned for heat and cooking. Electricity comes through wires to provide power and light. Some homes make their own energy using sunlight. And batteries store energy to use later.

7 **Solar panels** collect energy from sunshine and turn it into electricity. The electricity from the solar panels travels to the machines in the house by wires. Sunlight will never run out, so solar energy is called a renewable energy.

1 A maze of connections links your home to energy from the outside world. **Electrical cables** bring in electricity from power stations far away.

8 radio

3 electric guitar

2 **Telephone lines** snake behind walls.

4 **Gas pipes** flow under the street and to the house. Gas is used as fuel for heating and cooking.

6 telephone

LOOK INSIDE

Find the energy connections that power the machines in this house.

5 A **gas oven** burns gas as fuel. The oven uses gas to make thermal, or heat, energy to heat up your dinner.

10 A **satellite dish** on the roof picks up electrical signals and information from space.

👁 **FIND IT** INSIDE AND OUTSIDE

You'll need the magic lens to find some of these objects.

1 electrical cables   **8** radio

2 telephone lines   **9** electric toothbrush

3 electric guitar   **10** satellite dish

4 gas pipes   **11** computer

5 gas oven   **12** mobile phone

6 telephone   **13** television

7 solar panels   **14** bicycle

9 electric toothbrush

11 computer

What energy pulls an apple and everything else towards the ground? Gravity, or gravitational energy. Splat!

mobile phone with charger **12**

13 television

Cables connect the TV to the satellite dish so it can receive a signal.

14 When you push the pedals on a **bicycle**, you make kinetic energy, or the energy of movement. The pedals turn and you are on your way.

11

IN THE KITCHEN

What happens inside a machine?

Flick the 'On' switch and CLICK, POP, PING! Water boils in the kettle, bread toasts in the toaster and your porridge is piping hot from the microwave.

When energy flows through a machine, a marvellous chain reaction happens. Cogs, catches and wheels move into action, working together to get the job done.

Why does a toaster pop up?

Inside a toaster, electricity heats a wire, called a **filament**, which toasts slices of bread. When the bread is toasted, a timer triggers a **catch** to let go. Up pops the toast.

LOOK INSIDE

Find out what happens inside a machine that's turned on and working.

bread pops up

lever

catch

Electricity travels through a plug from wires behind the wall to power the many machines in the kitchen.

filament

How does a kettle work?

Inside an electric kettle, at the bottom of the **jug**, there is a **metal coil**. Electricity heats the coil, which boils the water. When the water gets hot enough, the lever flicks up and the kettle clicks off.

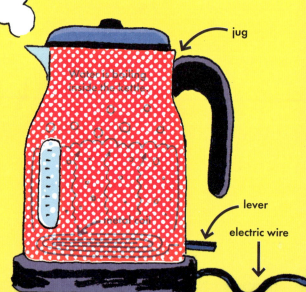

jug

Water is boiling inside the kettle

metal coil

lever

electric wire

What powers an oven?

Most ovens run on electricity, which heats up a filament, just like a toaster. In a convection oven, a fan blows **hot air** around the oven to cook the food. Dinner is ready.

How does a fridge stay cold?

Brr! To chill your food, a fridge moves heat around! Inside, a special liquid in pipes absorbs heat, which is then released at the back of the fridge into the kitchen. The special liquid is called a 'refrigerant'. When refrigerant absorbs heat, it turns into a gas. When it releases heat, it turns back into a liquid.

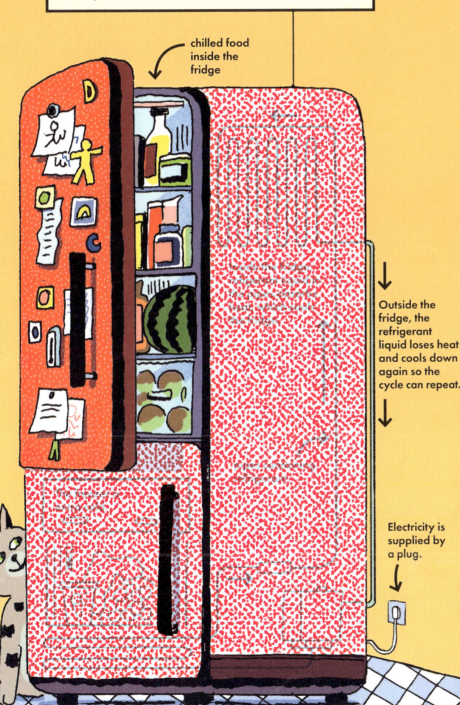

chilled food inside the fridge

Outside the fridge, the refrigerant liquid loses heat and cools down again so the cycle can repeat.

Electricity is supplied by a plug.

How did the 'microwave' get its name?

A microwave heats up food using rays of energy called 'microwaves'. Inside, the rays bounce around and when they hit the food, they heat it up. At the end of the cooking time, the timer goes ping.

timer

Is a hand whisk a machine?

Yes, it's a simple machine. You provide the energy to help beat air into your breakfast pancakes. Phew!

elbow power

TELEPHONE

How does your voice travel through thin air?

As if by magic, without a single cable or wire, a mobile phone carries your voice to a friend on a mobile far away, even in another country.

Radio waves provide the science behind the magic. We can't see, hear or feel radio waves, but they are all around us, zip zapping through the air extremely fast, sending and receiving messages.

LOOK INSIDE

Follow the invisible journey of the sound of voices on an international phone call.

Hello... hello...

1 Today, every day, twenty-four hours a day, across the world, we make millions of **mobile phone** calls to each other. Your mobile phone is similar to a two-way radio. It can make and receive calls from all kinds of places.

3 A part of the phone called the **antenna** turns the electrical signal into radio waves, which it beams into the air.

2 When you chat on a mobile phone, a tiny **microphone** turns the ups and downs of your voice into an up-and-down electrical signal.

4 The radio wave is sent to the nearest **communication tower**. The tower has antennae that work like ears to catch the waves. Once it's picked up the radio waves, it sends them bouncing from tower to tower and then to your friend's mobile phone.

👁 FIND IT
INSIDE AND OUTSIDE
You'll need the magic lens to find some of these objects.

1 mobile phone
2 microphone
3 antenna
4 communication tower

How does a microphone work?
When you speak, **sound waves** created by your voice carry energy towards the microphone.

Inside the microphone, there is a thin disc, called a **diaphragm**. When energy from the sound waves reaches the diaphragm, it vibrates, or moves backwards and forwards. These vibrations are converted into an **electrical signal** that can then be recorded or made louder.

Vibrations are converted into a signal by a magnet.

diaphragm

sound waves

How you doing?

The antenna in your friend's phone receives the radio waves. The speaker changes the up-and-down electrical signals back into your voice. You can both speak and listen to one another.

BICYCLE

How many bikes are there in the world?

Billions. A bike is simple to use and repair. It's clean and green, too. There's no pollution. Pedal power is the perfect way to make a short trip across town.

Push the pedals to turn the chain to make the wheels spin and off you go. You provide the force to start the bike and the energy to keep it going. This simple, two-wheeled design lets you stay upright and not fall off!

LOOK INSIDE

Find out what happens when you push the pedals, change the gears and press the breaks on a bike.

4 handlebars

2 front wheel

back wheel **3**

1 pedal

5 chain

6 gears

How do bicycle gears work?

A **chain** loops around **gears** – circles with teeth – which are attached to the pedals and the back wheel of the bike. When you push down on the pedals it pulls on the chain, which turns the back wheel and makes you go. When you change gear, you alter the way the pedals connect with the gears and the chain, which in turn makes the front and back wheels spin at different spee[...] Changing gear makes it easier to climb u[...] speed down a hill or ride quickly on the fl[...]

front gears

chain

back gears

8 bike helmet

7 scooter

👁 **FIND IT** INSIDE AND OUTSIDE

You'll need the magic lens to find some of these objects.

1. pedal
2. front wheel
3. back wheel
4. handlebars
5. chain
6. gears
7. scooter
8. crash helmet
9. brakes
10. skateboard

How do bicycle brakes work?

When you press the brakes, the **hand lever** pulls on a cable that runs from the handlebars to the wheel. **Brake pads** on either side of the wheel press against the wheel and the bike slows down, then stops.

hand lever

brake cable

brake pad

9 brakes

10 skateboard

17

ON THE ROAD

How do you start a car?

Turn the key in the ignition, handbrake off, press the accelerator and off the car goes. An engine helps the wheels to turn, then to pick up speed.

Right now, engines are powering all kinds of vehicles all over the world. Cars cruise down country lanes and nip up city streets, trucks rumble along motorways and racing cars speed around a racing track.

What makes a car go?

Most cars burn petrol, which is a fuel, but burning petrol causes pollution. Toxic, or poisonous, fumes from the engine spill out from the exhaust pipe into the air we breathe.

The steering wheel can be on different sides of the car depending on where you are driving in the world.

LOOK INSIDE

Explore what's under the bonnet of a car.

Why does a big truck have so many wheels?

To keep the heavy load in the large trailer
balanced, a truck can have over 18 wheels.

What makes a car move?

1 When you turn the ignition,
it powers up the battery,
which is connected to a
spark plug. Inside the engine,
the 'spark plug' makes a
powerful spark Zap!

2 The spark ignites fuel inside the
engine. The tiny explosion pushes
on a moving part, called a piston,
causing it to turn.

3 The pistons turn the axle,
which is attached to the wheels.
The car is on the move.

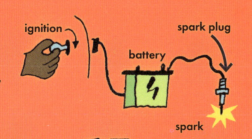

ignition

battery

spark plug

spark

piston

wheel

axle

How does an electric car work?

An electric car has a motor powered by a battery,
rather than an engine powered by fuel. In an electric
car, the battery is plugged into a charger. An electric car
doesn't pollute as much because it doesn't burn petrol.

AEROPLANE

How many planes are up in the air?

Right now, high up in the sky, an average of nearly 10,000 planes are criss-crossing above the Earth. They zip between airports around the world.

So, while you read this, at least one million people are snoozing, snacking and watching films as they zoom through the air at high speeds, far above the ground.

LOOK INSIDE

What happens inside the parts of a plane you usually can't see?

1 In the **cockpit**, the pilot and co-pilot fly the plane.

2 A **radar system** in the nose of the plane helps the pilot to check the weather and to keep track of the best route.

3 Before a flight, a **fuel truck** refuels the jumbo jet. The fuel powers the engines for the flight ahead.

4 It takes over an hour to pump fuel into the big tanks inside a plane's **hollow wings**.

jet engine **5**

6 A powerful jet engine whirrs into life. A large spinning **fan** sucks air into the engine, where flames of burning fuel heat it up. Then the air is pushed with tremendous force out of the back of the engine to move the plane forwards.

How does a plane take off?

The engine thrusts the plane forward at top speed. As the plane moves forward, air flows over the wings creating a force called lift. When there is enough lift to overcome the pull of gravity, the plane takes off and flies.

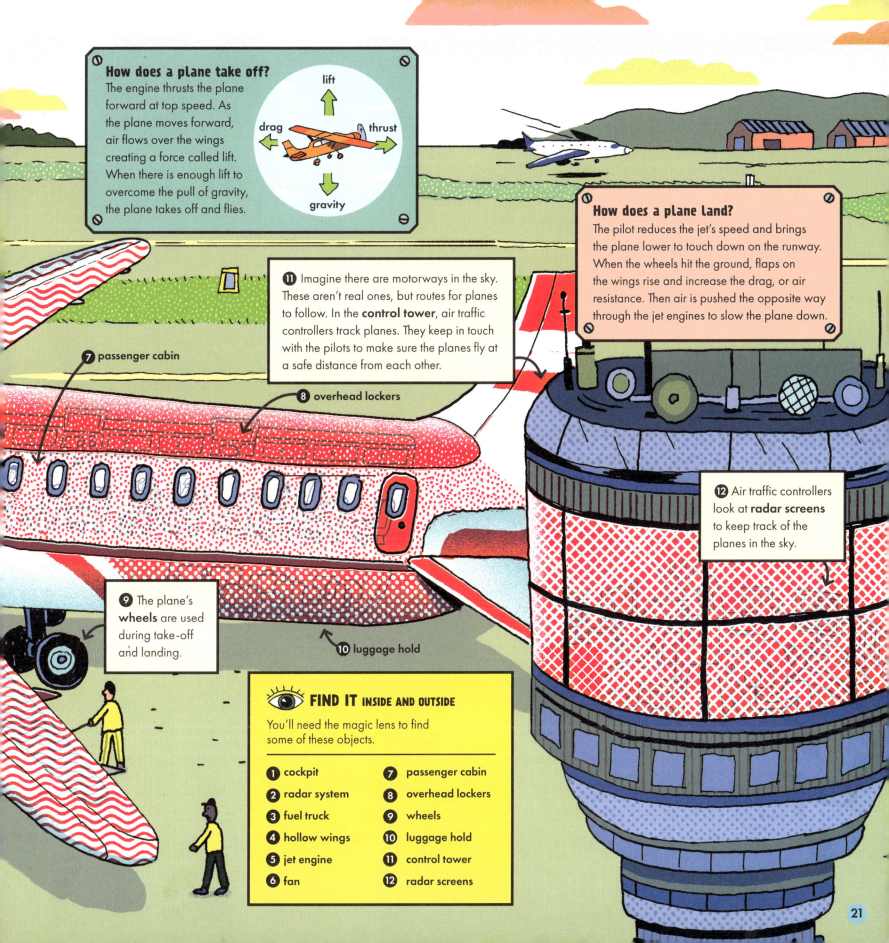

lift

drag

thrust

gravity

How does a plane land?

The pilot reduces the jet's speed and brings the plane lower to touch down on the runway. When the wheels hit the ground, flaps on the wings rise and increase the drag, or air resistance. Then air is pushed the opposite way through the jet engines to slow the plane down.

11 Imagine there are motorways in the sky. These aren't real ones, but routes for planes to follow. In the **control tower**, air traffic controllers track planes. They keep in touch with the pilots to make sure the planes fly at a safe distance from each other.

7 passenger cabin

8 overhead lockers

12 Air traffic controllers look at **radar screens** to keep track of the planes in the sky.

9 The plane's **wheels** are used during take-off and landing.

10 luggage hold

👁 **FIND IT** INSIDE AND OUTSIDE

You'll need the magic lens to find some of these objects.

1 cockpit
2 radar system
3 fuel truck
4 hollow wings
5 jet engine
6 fan
7 passenger cabin
8 overhead lockers
9 wheels
10 luggage hold
11 control tower
12 radar screens

MAGLEV TRAIN

How fast can a maglev train go?

This supersonic, almost silent train purrs along at up to 600 kilometres per hour. That's almost as fast as an aeroplane. The maglev cuts journey times in half.

The maglev is powered by the force of magnets. The word 'maglev' comes from two words – 'magnetic', which is a type of force, and 'levitate', which means to hover.

1 At first the train runs on wheels, then a set of **magnets on the bottom of the train** takes over. The magnets are cooled to -267 degrees Celsius, which is far below freezing. The magnets help the train to hover just above the track.

2 The magnets on the train attract, which means pull together, or repel, which means push apart, **magnets on the track**. Magnets at the back of the train repel. Magnets at the front of the train attract. This pulls the train forward. The forces from the magnets keep the train stable.

How do the maglev magnets work?

The maglev train is powered by magnets on the train and track. Every magnet has two poles, or ends, called a north pole (N) and a south pole (S). A north pole attracts a south pole and they pull together. A north pole repels, or pushes away, another north pole. This force makes the train levitate and move along the track.

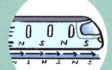

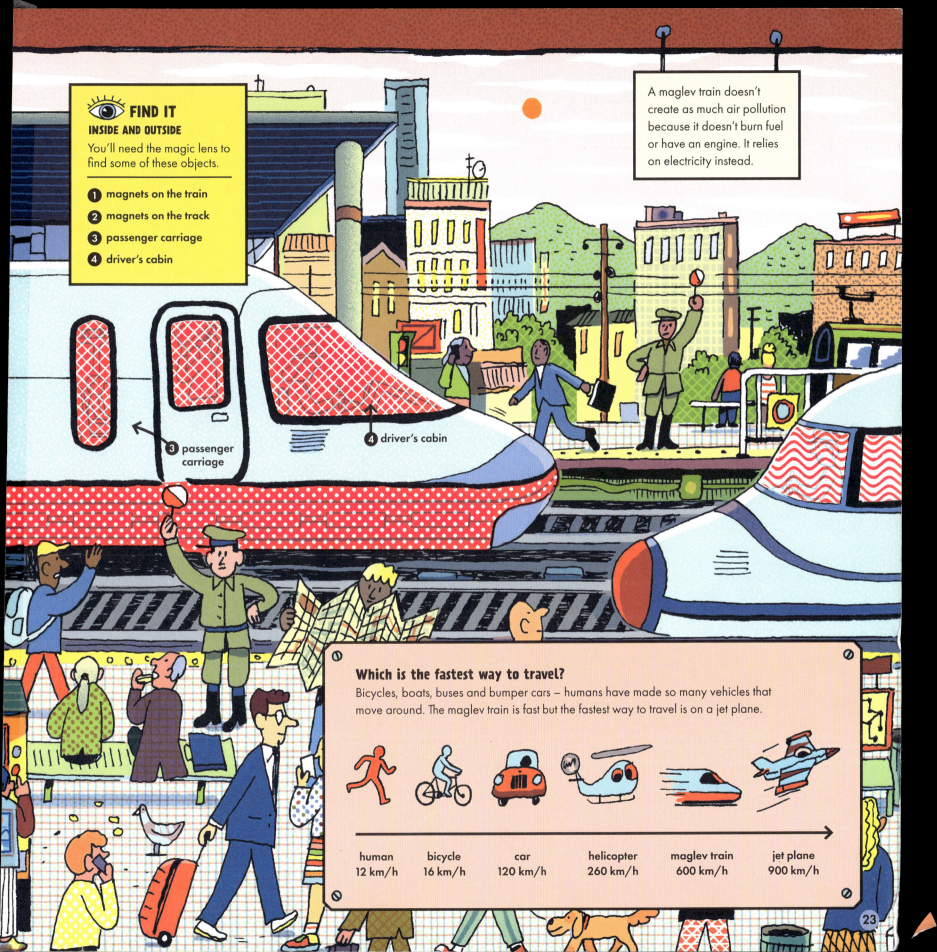

FIND IT

INSIDE AND OUTSIDE

You'll need the magic lens to find some of these objects.

1 magnets on the train
2 magnets on the track
3 passenger carriage
4 driver's cabin

A maglev train doesn't create as much air pollution because it doesn't burn fuel or have an engine. It relies on electricity instead.

3 passenger carriage

4 driver's cabin

Which is the fastest way to travel?

Bicycles, boats, buses and bumper cars – humans have made so many vehicles that move around. The maglev train is fast but the fastest way to travel is on a jet plane.

human	bicycle	car	helicopter	maglev train	jet plane
12 km/h	16 km/h	120 km/h	260 km/h	600 km/h	900 km/h

CONTAINER SHIP

How far does a container ship travel?

From one side of the world to the other. After more than a month at sea, a huge ship, chock-full of containers packed with goods, docks at port.

Each container is a truck-sized metal box filled with all sorts, from the latest computers to tins of beans. Inside the ship and on the deck, the containers stack neatly, one on top of the other, like gigantic building blocks.

LOOK INSIDE

Find out what happens above and below deck on a container ship.

3 From the **bridge**, the captain tracks the ship's course using computers.

4 deck

KARABOUDJAN

2 engine room

1 A small **tug boat** with a powerful outboard, or outside, motor helps guide the vast container ships to the dock.

How does a ship float?

In the water, two forces act on the ship. The force of gravity pulling the ship down is called the weight. The force of the water pushing it up is called upthrust. Because the ship has a wide shape, there is a lot of upthrust from the water. Even though the ship is heavy, it floats because its weight is balanced by the upthrust from the water.

weight ↓

↑ ↑ ↑ ↑ ↑ ↑

upthrust

7 Hoist away! A container hangs from a hook on a **crane**.

8 At the top of the crane, a **pulley wheel** holds the cable firm. Pulleys help to reduce the force needed to lift a load.

9 The crane's long arm is called a **jib**. It can swing from side to side and up and down.

10 A **counterweight** helps balance the crane and stops it from toppling over.

6 containers

👁 **FIND IT** INSIDE AND OUTSIDE

You'll need the magic lens to find some of these objects.

1 tug boat
2 engine room
3 bridge
4 deck
5 hull
6 containers
7 crane
8 pulley wheel
9 jib
10 counterweight
11 container trucks

5 The ship's **hull** is the main part of the ship that sits in the water and keeps it afloat. Hulls come in different shapes, from sleek, fast designs, to wide, stable hulls like this one.

11 Container trucks wait in a line for the towering crane to whirr into action. Each container is unloaded into the port and then put on a truck. Soon the trucks will be on the road delivering the goods to warehouses and shops up and down the country.

25

SUBMARINE

Why is a submarine shaped like a fish?

A submarine's long, slim shape, smooth sides and pointed nose help it speed silently through the water. A spinning propeller powers it forward – fast.

The crew climbs on board through a single hatch at the top, which slams shut from the inside. Two metal hulls, or outer coverings, help keep every drop of water out. The submarine is now sealed tight and ready to dive.

LOOK INSIDE

Discover what happens beneath the waves on a submarine.

2 Before the submarine dives, and when it surfaces, a **periscope** helps the crew to see above the waves.

3 The crew is protected from the strong water pressure of the ocean by two **hulls**, an inner and an outer one.

hatch **4**

5 engine room

1 A spinning **propeller** pushes the submarine through the water.

How does a submarine dive?

In the control room, the captain orders the crew to let water into the gap between the inner and the outer hulls. Water is heavier than air so the submarine sinks.

outer hull

inner hull

To rise to the surface, the crew blasts air back into the gap. The air pushes the water out and the submarine rises.

FIND IT INSIDE AND OUTSIDE

You'll need the magic lens to find some of these objects.

1 propeller   **8** crew's quarters
2 periscope   **9** breathing tank
3 hulls   **10** undersea cables
4 hatch   **11** ROV
5 engine room   **12** ocean research
6 control room   **13** ship diving bell
7 sonar

6 The captain steers from the **control room** with a computer system.

7 The crew uses a system called **sonar** to navigate. Sonar uses under water sound waves to tell how far away objects are in the sea.

8 The submarine crew sleeps in bunk beds in the **crew's quarters**. They can spend up to three months under water. It's a tight squeeze.

breathing tank **9**

10 From shore to shore, thousands of kilometres of **undersea cables** and pipes snake across the seabed. The cables help to send data, or information, around the world. Energy, such as gas, flows through the pipes.

11 Underwater, there are jobs to do. An **ROV**, which stands for Remotely Operated Vehicle, scoots around taking photographs to map the seabed. It also mends machinery with its mechanical arms.

12 The ROV is connected to an **ocean research ship** by a cable. The ship's crew instructs the ROV what to do, step by step.

13 A diver sits in a **diving bell** attached to a ship. The bell drops towards the seabed, protecting the diver from the water pressure outside. Then the diver swims out of the diving bell into the ocean through a hatch. The diver breathes with supplies from a tank.

UP AND DOWN IN THE CITY

What keeps a city on the move?

Machines keep a city moving, from a lift climbing to the top of a skyscraper, to an escalator looping under the street to the metro station below.

It's rush hour! Horns beep and traffic stops and starts at traffic lights. Far beneath the walking feet of workers, tourists and schoolchildren, the city is also busy with machines working underground.

1 helicopter

2 helicopter landing pad

3 passenger jet plane

👁 FIND IT INSIDE AND OUTSIDE

You'll need the magic lens to find some of these objects.

1 helicopter
2 helicopter landing pad
3 passenger jet plane
4 recycling truck
5 water pipes and sewers
6 utility tunnels

7 Internet connection
8 lift shaft
9 metro trains
10 automatic train doors
11 escalator
12 electric bicycle

4 Keep your city tidy! Every day, thousands of bags of rubbish are collected. Some of them are thrown into a **recycling truck** with a tipper at the back, then taken to the refuse centre to be sorted for recycling.

electric bicycle 12

LOOK INSIDE

Find out what happens above and below the city streets.

5 A maze of underground pipes and tunnels criss-crosses under the city. In and out, 24 hours a day, pipes bring in **water** and **sewers** take away waste.

7 Fibre-optic cables underground provide **Internet connections** across the city.

6 Pipes and cables run underground through a network of **utility tunnels**.

How does a lift work?

The lift car sits in a shaft and moves up and down between floors. At the top of the shaft, there is a machine room with a big motor.

motor

machine room

lift car

weight

lift shaft

When you press 'up', the motor pulls a strong wire cable attached to the lift over a pulley. At the same time, a weight pulls down to help balance the weight of the lift. The lift starts to rise. When you press 'down', the motor pulls the wire in the other direction and the lift goes down.

lift shaft **8**

12 electric bicycle

9 Don't miss your metro stop! Hop on and off **metro trains**, which run along tracks charged with electricity.

10 At each station, the driver opens and closes the **automatic train doors** with a computer.

11 Walk or stand, up and down, an **escalator** keeps everyone on the move. This looping staircase is powered by a motor, which moves a set of gears. Inside, a chain moves each step so it loops around to make a moving platform to stand on.

AT THE DOCTOR'S

How does a doctor see inside your body?

Open wide! A doctor looks into your mouth to see if your throat is sore, but what about the hidden parts of your body, deep inside?

Machines take pictures of bones and soft parts of the body, called organs. There are machines that pick up sounds to help a doctor tell what's happening inside your body, too.

ultrasound image

scanner

doctor

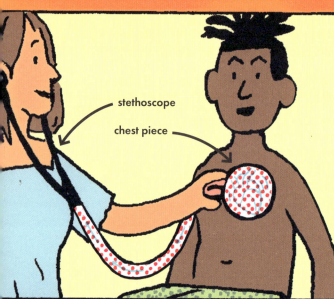

stethoscope

chest piece

How does a doctor hear your heart?

The doctor puts the **chest piece** of the **stethoscope** to your heart. The beating of your heart makes a disc of plastic in the chest piece, called a diaphragm, wobble or vibrate. The vibrations travel up the tube to the headset, where the doctor hears clearly.

How do sounds turn into pictures of a baby?

A doctor rubs a **scanner** called a transducer on the mum-to-be's stomach. Sound waves, or ultrasound, travel through soft parts, such as skin, but when the rays hit the baby growing, they bounce, or echo. The echoing sound waves build up what's called an **ultrasound** image.

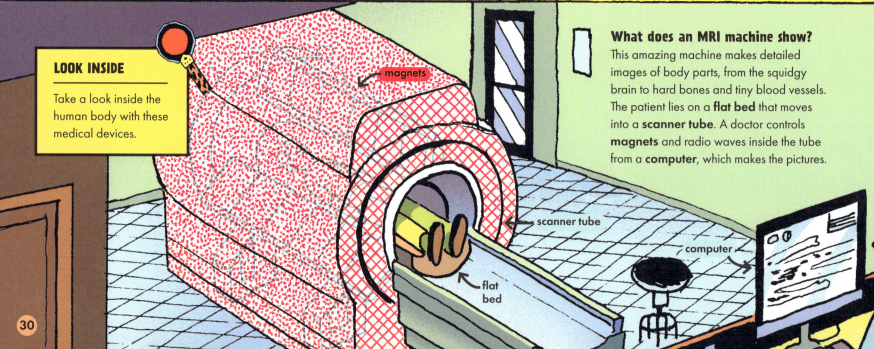

LOOK INSIDE

Take a look inside the human body with these medical devices.

magnets

What does an MRI machine show?

This amazing machine makes detailed images of body parts, from the squidgy brain to hard bones and tiny blood vessels. The patient lies on a **flat bed** that moves into a **scanner tube**. A doctor controls **magnets** and radio waves inside the tube from a **computer**, which makes the pictures.

scanner tube

computer

flat bed

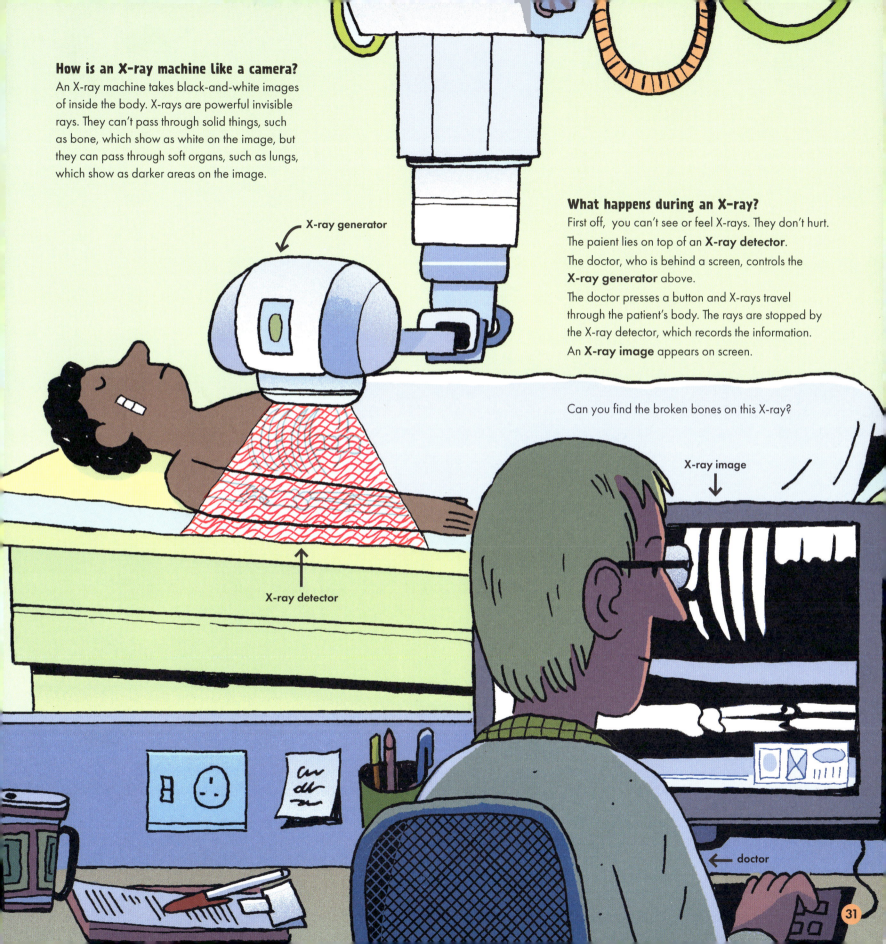

How is an X-ray machine like a camera?

An X-ray machine takes black-and-white images of inside the body. X-rays are powerful invisible rays. They can't pass through solid things, such as bone, which show as white on the image, but they can pass through soft organs, such as lungs, which show as darker areas on the image.

X-ray generator

What happens during an X-ray?

First off, you can't see or feel X-rays. They don't hurt.

The paient lies on top of an **X-ray detector**.

The doctor, who is behind a screen, controls the **X-ray generator** above.

The doctor presses a button and X-rays travel through the patient's body. The rays are stopped by the X-ray detector, which records the information.

An **X-ray image** appears on screen.

Can you find the broken bones on this X-ray?

X-ray image

X-ray detector

doctor

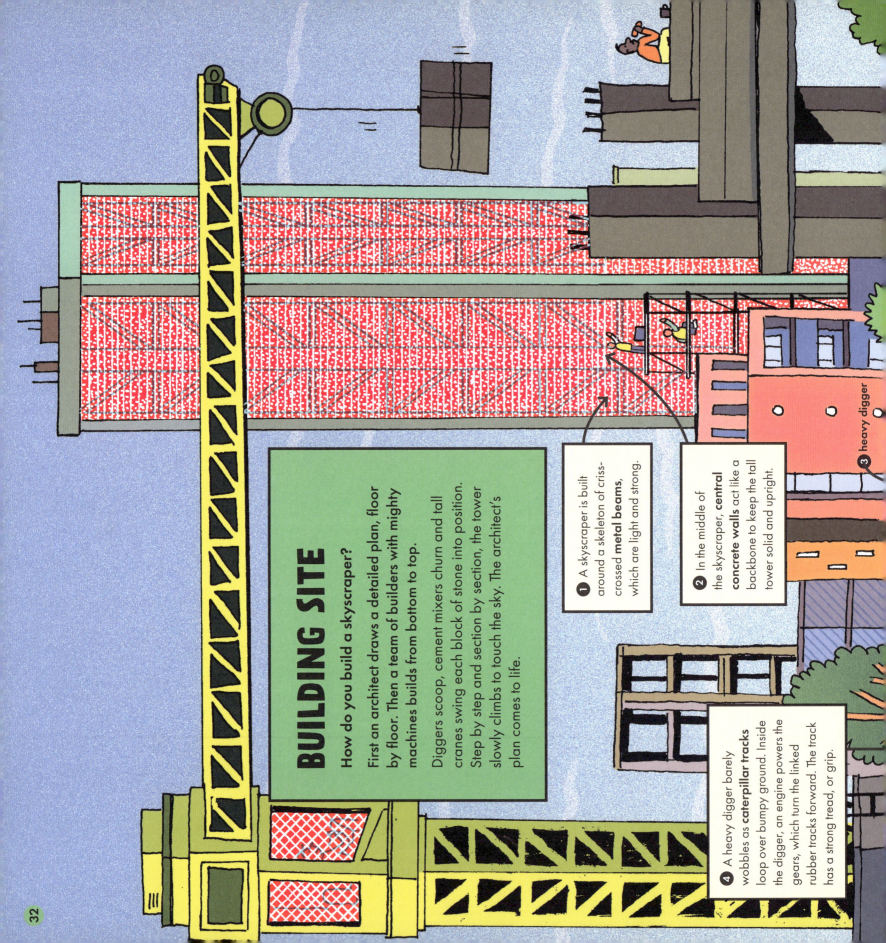

BUILDING SITE

How do you build a skyscraper?

First an architect draws a detailed plan, floor by floor. Then a team of builders with mighty machines builds from bottom to top.

Diggers scoop, cement mixers churn and tall cranes swing each block of stone into position. Step by step and section by section, the tower slowly climbs to touch the sky. The architect's plan comes to life.

1 A skyscraper is built around a skeleton of criss-crossed **metal beams**, which are light and strong.

2 In the middle of the skyscraper, **central concrete walls** act like a backbone to keep the tall tower solid and upright.

3 heavy digger

4 A heavy digger barely wobbles as **caterpillar tracks** loop over bumpy ground. Inside the digger, an engine powers the gears, which turn the linked rubber tracks forward. The track has a strong tread, or grip.

9 pneumatic drill

👁 FIND IT INSIDE AND OUTSIDE
You'll need the magic lens to find some of these objects.

1. metal beams
2. central concrete walls
3. heavy digger
4. caterpillar tracks
5. bucket
6. cement mixer
7. cement chute
8. concrete
9. pneumatic drill
10. foundations

10 Before a tower can go up, builders have to dig down. **Foundations** give the building a solid base to sit on. They are made of a thick layer of concrete and stop the heavy tower sinking into the soft soil or falling over in high winds. The foundations anchor the tower to the ground like a tree's roots.

5 The digger scoops up rubble using a **bucket** with a sharp blade on its edge.

7 When the concrete is needed, blades turn towards a **cement chute**, which tips out the sloppy wet mixture.

8 concrete

6 Inside a **cement mixer**, concrete is made in the drum, which spins to stop a mixture of cement, sand and water from going hard.

What's earthquake architecture?
In many countries, architects design buildings to stay up during earthquakes. These buildings are designed to wobble, or vibrate, slightly. When there are powerful winds or the earth shifts, the buildings bend rather than break.

PRINTING PRESS

How do you print a book?

Most books are printed on a huge machine, called a printing press. Then they are sent by a container ship, train or truck to where you live or a bookshop nearby.

To print the billions of books in the world, you need three things – ink, paper and a printing press. It's called a 'printing press' because the paper is pressed against the ink so the words and pictures print on the paper.

How is a book made?

1 The publisher sets up a **creative team** to work on the book. The author writes. The illustrator draws. The designer makes computer files of the cover and pages. And the editor and expert make sure everything is clear and correct.

2 computer

LOOK INSIDE

Discover how the pages of a book are printed.

3 The computer files are sent to the printing company for the words and pictures to be printed on a **printing press**.

4 A huge stack of sheets of **paper** is fed into the printing press.

5 The paper passes through four sections and each one prints one colour with **coloured ink** – cyan (C), magenta (M), yellow (Y) and black (K). First the sheets are printed on one side, then they are fed back into the machine to print on the other side.

C   CM   CMY   CMYK

What's four-colour printing?

The colourful pictures in a book can be printed with just four colours. The colours used are:

- ● cyan, which is blue
- ● magenta, which is pink
- ● yellow
- ● black

The range, or spectrum, of other colours is made by printing different amounts of the four colours, one on top of the other.

Orange colours are made with magenta and lots of yellow. What about the green colours?

6 Next the printed sheets are folded into sections of eight pages, called signatures. Then the signatures are trimmed and all of them are sewn together along one edge. These steps are done by a series of **fold, trim and bind machines**.

7 The cover is stuck onto a hard board. To finish, the pages are glued to the spine on the cover. The **finished book** is ready.

FIND IT INSIDE AND OUTSIDE

You'll need the magic lens to find some of these objects.

1. creative team
2. computer
3. printing press
4. paper
5. coloured ink
6. fold, trim and bind machines
7. finished book

Take the book challenge

Find clues at the front of this book about how it was made.

- What year was this book created?
- What's the name of the publisher who made this book?
- Every book has its own special number, called an International Standard Book Number, or ISBN. What's the ISBN for this book?

ROBOTS

Will robots take over the world?

Robots are everywhere today – in factories, hospitals and even up in space observing the Earth. A robot can be a massive machine or a pin-sized microbot.

A robot is programmed to follow computer instructions to perform a task, so it can't really make decisions itself or take over the world. Robots do extremely precise, dangerous, heavy-duty, tiring and boring jobs. Sometimes these are jobs that people can't or don't want to do themselves.

robot

camera

computer

LOOK INSIDE

Discover what happens behind the nuts and bolts of a robot.

Robot versus human

Often in films, robots walk and talk like humans, but they are machines not people. A robot doesn't have independent thoughts or feelings. It is controlled by a **computer** not a brain. It doesn't see with eyes or hear with ears but with a **camera** and **microphone** instead. Humanoid robots look like humans and can be programmed to act like people but they are still robots.

grippable jointed fingers

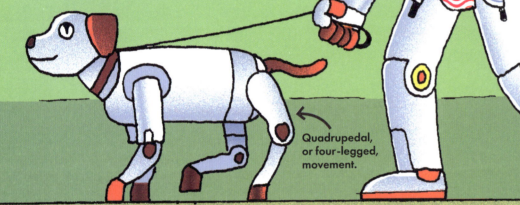

Quadrupedal, or four-legged, movement.

Bipedal, or two-legged, movement, similar to a human being.

How do robots build cars?

In a car factory, big robots work together on a production line. First a robot joins together pieces to make the car **chassis**, or frame.

One robot cuts metal sheets into doors, then joins, or rivets, them to the chassis. Another robot performs detailed work on the engine.

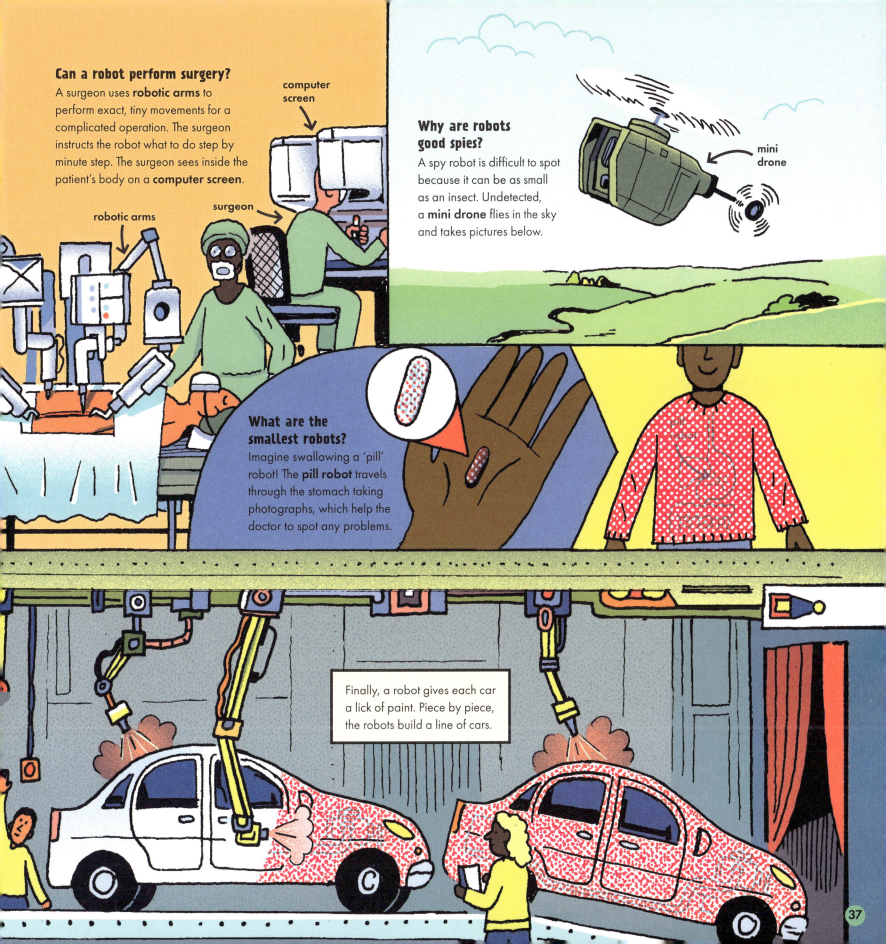

Can a robot perform surgery?

A surgeon uses **robotic arms** to perform exact, tiny movements for a complicated operation. The surgeon instructs the robot what to do step by minute step. The surgeon sees inside the patient's body on a **computer screen**.

computer screen

robotic arms

surgeon

Why are robots good spies?

A spy robot is difficult to spot because it can be as small as an insect. Undetected, a **mini drone** flies in the sky and takes pictures below.

mini drone

What are the smallest robots?

Imagine swallowing a 'pill' robot! The **pill robot** travels through the stomach taking photographs, which help the doctor to spot any problems.

Finally, a robot gives each car a lick of paint. Piece by piece, the robots build a line of cars.

TELESCOPE

How far into space can we see?

Out of this world! High up in the sky, the Hubble Space Telescope shows us pictures from far beyond the planets circling the Sun, called our Solar System.

Meanwhile on the ground, in the darkness of night, astronomers, point their telescopes upwards to study light from stars and planets. The astronomers record details of faraway space.

1 About every ninety-five minutes, the **Hubble Space Telescope** makes a curved path, called an orbit, around Earth. It can see an object ten billion times fainter or further away than if a person looked just with their eyes. Hubble sits above the Earth's atmosphere, which blocks out some space light. This makes the images it sends back to Earth as radio waves really clear.

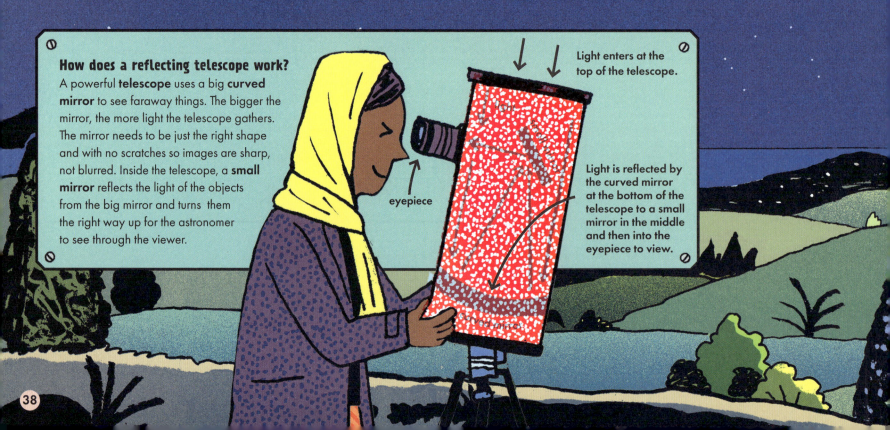

How does a reflecting telescope work?
A powerful **telescope** uses a big **curved mirror** to see faraway things. The bigger the mirror, the more light the telescope gathers. The mirror needs to be just the right shape and with no scratches so images are sharp, not blurred. Inside the telescope, a **small mirror** reflects the light of the objects from the big mirror and turns them the right way up for the astronomer to see through the viewer.

eyepiece

Light enters at the top of the telescope.

Light is reflected by the curved mirror at the bottom of the telescope to a small mirror in the middle and then into the eyepiece to view.

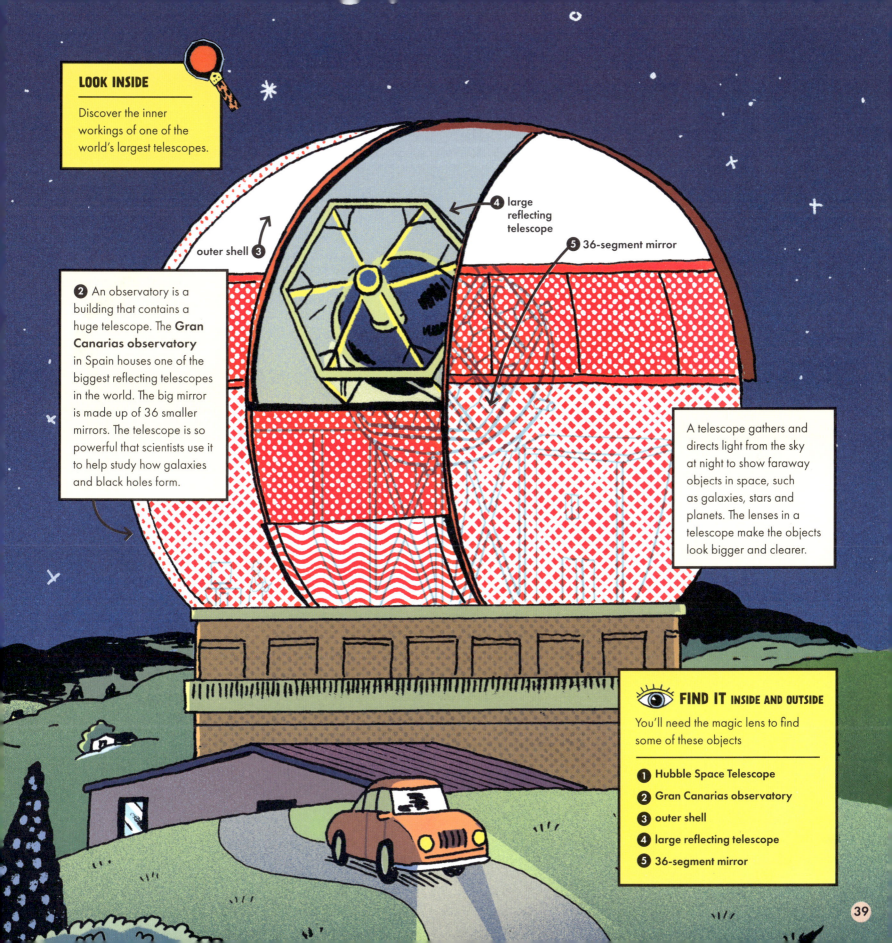

Discover the inner workings of one of the world's largest telescopes.

4 large reflecting telescope

outer shell **3**

5 36-segment mirror

2 An observatory is a building that contains a huge telescope. The **Gran Canarias observatory** in Spain houses one of the biggest reflecting telescopes in the world. The big mirror is made up of 36 smaller mirrors. The telescope is so powerful that scientists use it to help study how galaxies and black holes form.

A telescope gathers and directs light from the sky at night to show faraway objects in space, such as galaxies, stars and planets. The lenses in a telescope make the objects look bigger and clearer.

FIND IT INSIDE AND OUTSIDE
You'll need the magic lens to find some of these objects

1 Hubble Space Telescope
2 Gran Canarias observatory
3 outer shell
4 large reflecting telescope
5 36-segment mirror

The Dragon capsule continues on and docks with the **ISS**. The capsule carries supplies for the astronauts on board the space station.

At the same time, the second stage continues on its journey into space, and then releases the spacecraft, the Dragon capsule.

Engines kick in to reduce the first stage's speed, so it returns to Earth slower and slower, until four small legs touch the landing platform softly.

The rocket powers high into the Earth's atmosphere. The first stage separates and falls back to Earth.

MISSION COMPLETE

SECOND STAGE CONTINUES INTO SPACE

SEPARATION

ROCKET

How long does it take to fly into space?

Usually a rocket takes between eight and eleven minutes from lift-off to escaping the Earth's atmosphere, which is the band of air around our planet.

It also depends what you mean by 'space'. Some scientists say outer space is beyond the Moon. Humans haven't travelled past this point yet, and it takes about three days for humans just to reach the Moon.

6 The **payload** is the passengers and cargo, such as a satellite or supplies, that the rocket is taking up into space. The payload in this rocket is stored at the top in a spacecraft called the Dragon capsule.

A rocket propels, or drives, upwards into space. It takes its own fuel along and burns it in its engines for energy. In the past, rockets crashed back to Earth, but the Falcon 9 lands safely, ready to fly to space again and again.

5 second stage

LOOK INSIDE

Discover what's inside a rocket travelling into space.

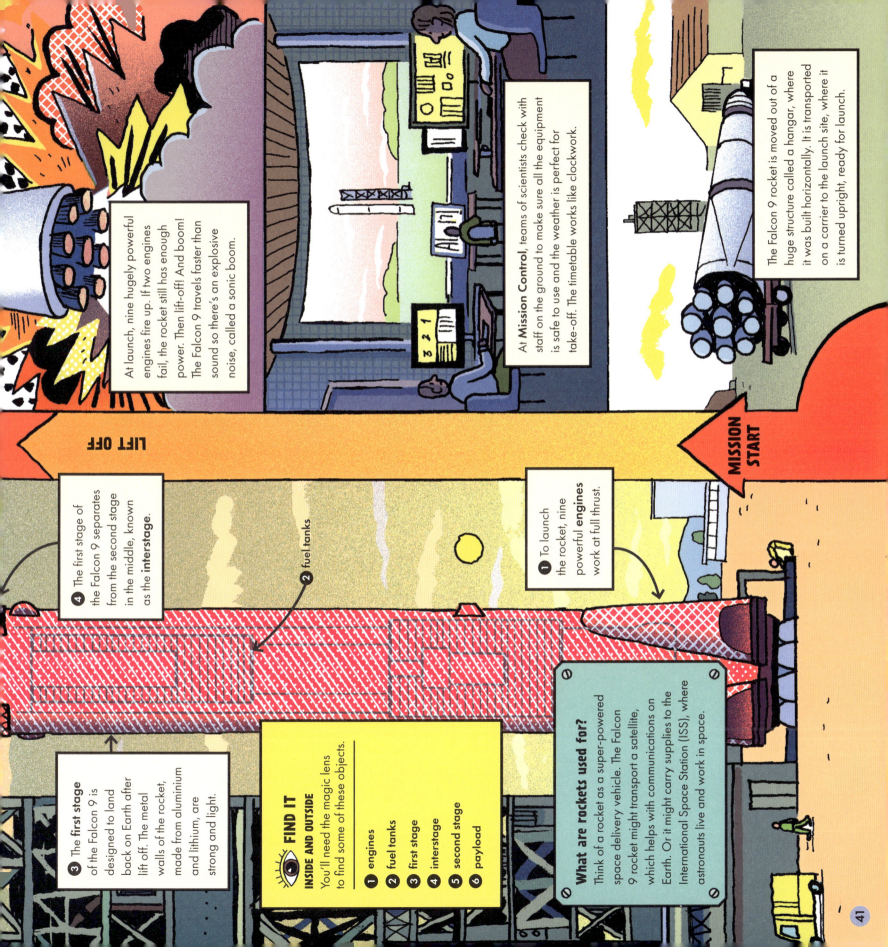

LIFT OFF

At launch, nine hugely powerful engines fire up. If two engines fail, the rocket still has enough power. Then lift-off! And boom! The Falcon 9 travels faster than sound so there's an explosive noise, called a sonic boom.

At **Mission Control**, teams of scientists check with staff on the ground to make sure all the equipment is safe to use and the weather is perfect for take-off. The timetable works like clockwork.

The Falcon 9 rocket is moved out of a huge structure called a hangar, where it was built horizontally. It is transported on a carrier to the launch site, where it is turned upright, ready for launch.

MISSION START

4 The **first stage** of the Falcon 9 separates from the second stage in the middle, known as the **interstage**.

2 fuel tanks

1 To launch the rocket, nine powerful **engines** work at full thrust.

3 The **first stage** of the Falcon 9 is designed to land back on Earth after lift-off. The metal walls of the rocket, made from aluminium and lithium, are strong and light.

👁 FIND IT
INSIDE AND OUTSIDE
You'll need the magic lens to find some of these objects.
1 engines
2 fuel tanks
3 first stage
4 interstage
5 second stage
6 payload

What are rockets used for?
Think of a rocket as a super-powered space delivery vehicle. The Falcon 9 rocket might transport a satellite, which helps with communications on Earth. Or it might carry supplies to the International Space Station (ISS), where astronauts live and work in space.

SPACE STATION

How do you brush your teeth in space?

The same way you do on Earth, with a toothbrush and toothpaste, but the trick is to stop globules of water and the toothpaste cap from floating away!

Just think, above your head and the clouds, a crew of astronauts lives on a mega-machine, called the International Space Station (ISS). This is a vast science laboratory high up in space, where there's no force of gravity to pull things down and stop them from floating away.

How does the ISS stay up in space?

Every day, about sixteen times a day, the ISS orbits, or makes a circle, above the Earth. It does not fall to Earth because it moves forward at exactly the correct speed to counter the force of gravity, which pulls it downwards. It travels on a curved path that matches the shape of the Earth.

solar array wings **6**

LOOK INSIDE

Find out what happens on board the ISS over a day.

1 A crew can spend over six months on the ISS. Usually astronauts are up by 6 am and in bed by 9:30 pm. Because there's no gravity in space, astronauts strap themselves into bed in **sleeping compartments** so that they don't float away. Each morning, there's a timetable of the jobs to do over the day.

2 An astronaut carries out **experiments**, including studying how plants grow in space. Astronauts also do medical experiments on each other to see how the body works in space and to develop new medicines.

7 main truss (support beam)

Columbus laboratory **8**

Harmony module **9**

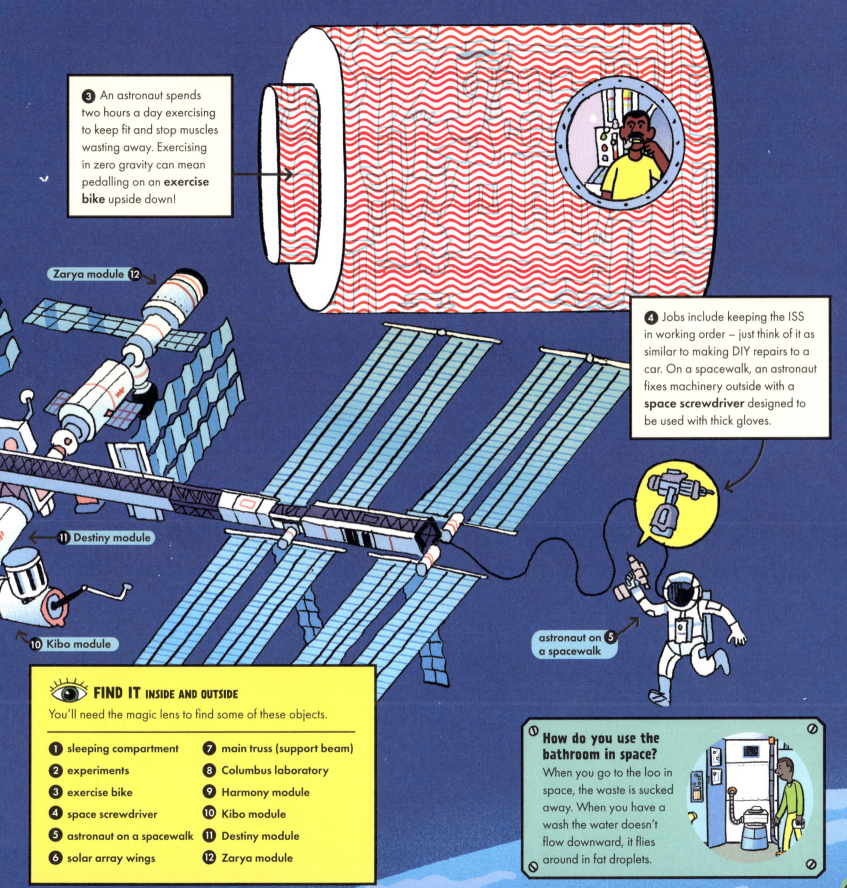

3 An astronaut spends two hours a day exercising to keep fit and stop muscles wasting away. Exercising in zero gravity can mean pedalling on an **exercise bike** upside down!

Zarya module **12**

4 Jobs include keeping the ISS in working order – just think of it as similar to making DIY repairs to a car. On a spacewalk, an astronaut fixes machinery outside with a **space screwdriver** designed to be used with thick gloves.

11 Destiny module

10 Kibo module

astronaut on **5**
a spacewalk

FIND IT INSIDE AND OUTSIDE
You'll need the magic lens to find some of these objects.

1 sleeping compartment   **7** main truss (support beam)
2 experiments   **8** Columbus laboratory
3 exercise bike   **9** Harmony module
4 space screwdriver   **10** Kibo module
5 astronaut on a spacewalk **11** Destiny module
6 solar array wings   **12** Zarya module

How do you use the bathroom in space?
When you go to the loo in space, the waste is sucked away. When you have a wash the water doesn't flow downward, it flies around in fat droplets.

MACHINES AND US

Machines can help people do all kinds of amazing things, from talking to a friend on the other side of the world to sending astronauts into space.

Why do people invent new machines?

To make life easier. Often machines help to do things much more quickly and easily. Making a car on a production line in a factory is much quicker than making one all by hand. And some machines allow humans to do things we just can't do alone. For example, a telescope helps us to see into space.

Who built the first machines?

Prehistoric people made simple tools with stone. Then, thousands of years ago in the Middle East, the wheel was invented. Wheels still help move people and things from place to place.

What will machines be able to do in the future?

The sky is the limit. Just think, over fifty years ago, there were no mobile phones. And over one hundred years ago, nobody had visited space. Imagine life one hundred years from now. What machines would you like to see in the world?

What machine would you like to invent?

You could invent a machine to solve a problem – maybe how not to get wet in the rain? Or maybe your machine does two things at once – it might wake you up and feed you breakfast! Think about a machine you would like to invent. Think big. How is it powered? What parts do you need to make it? And remember to stick with it. Often it takes a lot of experimentation to invent a machine that works.

Would you like to grow up to invent new machines?

Engineers devise most new machines. There are many jobs involved, from designing big machines – such as bridges, trains and space rockets – to programming computers and robots.

Next time you use a machine, think about what makes it work.

INDEX

SOURCE NOTES

Gaffney, K. *Simple Machines* (Oxford: Raintree, 2017)

'Simple Machines', Easy Science for Kids (easyscienceforkids.com)

'Simple machines', DK findout! (www.dkfindout.com)

Brain, M. *How Stuff Works* (New York: Hungry Minds, 2001)

How things work: the universal encyclopedia of machines trans. C. van Amerongen (London: Granada, 1972)

'Work and energy', Khan Academy (www.khanacademy.org)

'How Do Solar Panels Work?', Live Science (www.livescience.com)

'Fuel for thought: How does energy get to your home?', British Gas (www.britishgas.co.uk)

'How Satellite TV Works', How Stuff Works (www.howstuffworks.com)

'How Refrigerators Work', How Stuff Works (www.howstuffworks.com)

'How Do Microwaves Work?', Britannica (www.britannica.com)

'How Cell Phones Work', How Stuff Works (www.howstuffworks.com)

'How do mobile phones work?', physics.org (www.physics.org)

'Microphones', BBC Bitesize (www.bbc.co.uk/bitesize)

Hills, L. *The Bicycle* (MN, USA: Captsone Press, 2005)

Kelly, M. *Cars, Trucks and Bikes* (Thaxted, UK: Miles Kelly, 2010)

Porter, E. and Lozano, A. *Peeking under the bonnet* (Oxford: Raintree, 2016)

'The engine', How A Car Works (www.howacarworks.com)

'How Does a Jet engine Work?', MIT School of Engineering (engineering.mit.edu)

'How Air Traffic Control Works', Civil Aviation Authority (www.caa.co.uk)

'Maglev train', Britannica (www.britannica.com)

'Magnetic Fields and Lines', Physics LibreTexts (phys.libretexts.org)

'How maglev works', Phys.org (https://phys.org)

'What is a force?', BBC Bitesize (www.bbc.co.uk/bitesize)

'Force', Britannica Kids (kids.britannica.com)

'What is a magnet?', BBC Bitesize (www.bbc.co.uk/bitesize)

'Forces', BBC Bitesize (www.bbc.co.uk/bitesize)

'What is the Process of Docking a Container Ship?', More Than Shipping (www.morethanshipping.com)

'Journey of Your Container', More Than Shipping (www.morethanshipping.com)

'Introduction to Submarine Design', Marine Insight (www.marineinsight.com)

'How Submarines Work', How Stuff Works (www.howstuffworks.com)

'How are major undersea cables laid in the ocean?', *Independent* (www.independent.co.uk)

'What are Underwater ROVs & What are They Used For?', Deep Trekker (www.deeptrekker.com)

'Diving Bell', Britannica (www.britannica.com)

'New Designs Going Up—Working Knowledge on Elevators', Scientific American (www.scientificamerican.com)

'How M1 Tanks Work', How Stuff Works (www.howstuffworks.com)

'How Cement Mixers Work', How Stuff Works (www.howstuffworks.com)

'Skyscraper', Britannica (www.britannica.com)

'High Rise Buildings', Britannica (www.britannica.com)

'How Earthquake Resistant Buildings Work', How Stuff Works (www.howstuffworks.com)

'Stethoscope Science: Hearing Heart Rates', Scientific American (www.scientificamerican.com)

'Ultrasound Scan', NHS (www.nhs.co.uk)

'How does an MRI scanner work?', Science Focus (www.sciencefocus.com)

'X-Ray', NHS (www.nhs.co.uk)

'New Versius robot surgery system coming to NHS', BBC News (www.bbc.co.uk/news)

'Insect Spy Drone', Snopes (www.snopes.com)

Maran, S. P. *Astronomy for Dummies* (CA, USA: IDG, 1999)

'Telescope quick facts', NASA Hubblesite (hubblesite.org)

'Reflecting telescopes', DK findout! (www.dkfindout.com)

'Astronomical observatory', Britannica (www.britannica.com)

'Introducing the Gran Telescopio Canarias', Gran Telescopio CANARIAS (www.gtc.iac.es)

'Rockets and rocket launches, explained', National Geographic (www.nationalgeographic.com)

'SpaceX Falcon 9 rocket facts', Spaceflight Now (spaceflightnow.com)

'Falcon 9', SpaceX (www.spacex.com)

Gifford, C. *The International Space Station* (London: Wayland, 2017)

Stone, J. *Space Travel* (London: DK Children, 2019)

'International Space Station Facts and Figures', NASA (www.nasa.gov)

'The International Space Station', ESA Kids (www.esa.int)

'What is it like to sleep in space?', How Stuff Works (www.howstuffworks.com)